CW01642696

CENGAGE Learning

Novels for Students, Volume 20

Project Editors: Ira Mark Milne and Timothy Sisler **Editorial**: Anne Marie Hacht, Maikue Vang

Rights Acquisition and Management: Edna Hedblad, Sheila Spencer, Ann Taylor **Manufacturing**: Rhonda Williams

Imaging: Lezlie Light, Mike Logusz, Kelly A. Quin **Product Design**: Pamela A. E. Galbreath

Product Manager: Meggin Condino

For more information, contact
Thomson Gale
27500 Drake Rd.
Farmington Hills, MI 48331-3535
Or you can visit our Internet site at

Thomson Gale
27500 Drake Rd.
Farmington Hills, MI 48331-3535
Permissions Hotline: 248-699-8006 or 800-877-4253, ext. 8006
Fax: 248-699-8074 or 800-762-4058

corrected in future editions.

ISBN 0-7876-6943-1
ISSN 1094-3552

Printed in the United States of America
10 9 8 7 6 5 4 3 2 1

Hard Times

Charles Dickens

1854

Introduction

Hard Times, by Charles Dickens, was first published in serial form in the weekly magazine *Household Words*, from April to August of 1854. Set in fictional Coketown in the industrial north of England, the novel follows the fortunes of a variety of characters, including Thomas Gradgrind, who believes only in the utilitarian, "hard facts" school of thought; his dishonest son, Thomas; and his emotionally stifled daughter, Louisa. Other central characters are the boastful manufacturer, Josiah

Bounderby; the manipulative idler, James Harthouse; and the virtuous but persecuted worker, Stephen Blackpool; and his saintly friend, Rachel.

Dickens's purpose in *Hard Times* was to satirize the utilitarian philosophy that recognized only the value of human reason, neglecting not only what Dickens calls in the novel "fancy" but also the values of the human heart. Dickens also wanted to highlight the harsh, monotonous lives of factory workers and to criticize the laissez-faire economic philosophy of the marketplace.

Hard Times has not usually been regarded as one of Dickens's finest novels. While some critics do regard it highly, others argue that the characters do not fully come to life. According to this view, Dickens's didactic purpose stifled his comic genius and his ability to tell an entertaining story. Be that as it may, *Hard Times* remains a powerful exposure of the ills of nineteenth-century industrialism and the philosophy that turned a blind eye to its inadequacies and injustices.

Author Biography

One of England's greatest novelists, Charles Dickens was born in Landport, Hampshire, on February 7, 1812, the son of John and Elizabeth Dickens. In 1814, the family moved to London and then to Chatham, in Kent. John Dickens, a clerk in the Naval Pay Office, was imprisoned for debt in 1824, and Charles was sent to work in a shoe-blacking warehouse for five months.

After attending Wellington House Academy in London from 1824 to 1827, Dickens became a solicitor's clerk and studied shorthand. Within a few years he had become a freelance newspaper reporter, and he published his first short story in 1833. *Sketches by Boz*, his sketches of London life, was published in 1836, the same year he became editor of a new monthly magazine, *Bentley's Miscellany*, a post he held for three years. Dickens also married Catherine Hogarth in 1836. They were to produce ten children, but the couple separated in 1858.

Dickens then began publishing novels, all in serial form, at a prolific rate. His first novel was *The Pickwick Papers* (1836–1837), followed between 1837 and 1839 by *Oliver Twist* and *Nicholas Nickleby*. Next were *The Old Curiosity Shop* (1840–1841) and *Barnaby Rudge* (1841).

In 1842, Dickens toured the United States and Canada giving lectures in which he advocated the abolition of slavery. He published *American Notes* in October 1842. Over the remainder of the decade, Dickens wrote *Martin Chuzzlewit* (1843–1844), *A Christmas Carol* (1843), *Dombey and Son* (1846–1848), and *David Copperfield* (1849–1850).

In 1850, Dickens established the weekly magazine *Household Words*, which he edited and contributed to until it ceased publication in 1859. During the 1850s, Dickens published *Bleak House* (1852–1853), *Hard Times* (1854), and *Little Dorrit* (1855–1857). *A Tale of Two Cities* (1859) appeared in *All the Year Round*, a new weekly edited by Dickens.

In 1858, Dickens gave a series of public readings from his works in London and elsewhere. Public readings became a feature of Dickens's life throughout the 1860s, including a reading in Paris in 1863 and a tour of America, which began in December 1867, in Boston. That tour continued through to April 1868, in East Coast cities, in spite of the fact that Dickens was in poor health.

During the 1860s, Dickens published *Great Expectations* (1860–1861) and *Our Mutual Friend* (1864–1865). His last book, *The Mystery of Edwin Drood*, had begun publication but remained unfinished at the time of his death at Gadshill, near Rochester, Kent, on June 9, 1870, of a stroke.

Plot Summary

Book the First—Sowing

Hard Times begins in a classroom in the fictional English industrial town of Coketown, where Thomas Gradgrind is explaining his educational principles. He believes education should be based on facts and nothing else. On his way home, Gradgrind passes a circus and is shocked when he finds his two children, Thomas and Louisa, amusing themselves there. He scolds them and takes them home.

At Gradgrind's home, Bounderby is taking pride in explaining to Mrs. Gradgrind about his deprived childhood, when Gradgrind returns and worries about his children's interest in the circus. He and Bounderby decide this is probably because Cecilia (Sissy) Jupe, one of the pupils at the school, is the daughter of one of the circus men. Bounderby gives instructions for Sissy to be dismissed from the school.

Intending to meet Sissy's father, Gradgrind and Bounderby visit the circus folk at the Pegasus's Arms. But Sissy's father has deserted her. Gradgrind agrees with Mr. Sleary, the circus owner, to take Sissy into his own house and educate her.

Bounderby tells Mrs. Sparsit, his housekeeper, that he intends to employ young Tom Gradgrind after he has finished his education. Later, Tom tells Louisa he hates the education he has received. He plans to enjoy himself more when he lives with Bounderby because he knows Bounderby is fond of Louisa, and he plans to use that to his advantage. Meanwhile, Sissy finds it hard to settle down in her new life, with her education in facts alone. She waits every day for a letter from her father, but it never arrives.

Stephen Blackpool, a weaver at a local factory, meets his friend Rachel in the street and walks her home. When he returns to his own house, he finds that his drunken wife has returned to him again. Stephen makes an appointment with Bounderby and asks whether he can divorce his wife. Bounderby says he must live with the situation. On his way home, Stephen is accosted by a mysterious old woman, who asks him about Bounderby, offering no explanation of why she wants the information. When Stephen arrives home, he finds Rachel attending his wife, who has been injured. During the night his wife wakes up and almost drinks some poisonous medicine. Rachel stops her in the nick of time.

Some time passes. Tom goes to live with Bounderby; Gradgrind becomes a member of Parliament, and Bounderby marries Louisa, even though she does not love him. Bounderby then dismisses Mrs. Sparsit but gives her an apartment in the bank.

Book the Second—Reaping

Bitzer, the bank messenger, informs Mrs. Sparsit that he does not trust Tom. A well-dressed stranger arrives to speak to Mrs. Sparsit, inquiring about Bounderby and his wife. The stranger is James Harthouse, who has been trained in the "hard facts" school of political thought and sent to Coketown by Gradgrind. Harthouse befriends Tom and takes a liking to Louisa, whom he realizes does not love her husband.

A union representative, Slackbridge, gives a fiery speech to the factory hands, in which he condemns Stephen Blackpool for refusing to join their union. Stephen is thereafter scorned by the other factory hands, who refuse to speak to him.

Stephen is summoned to see Bounderby, who fires him, and Stephen decides he must leave town. The mysterious old woman visits Stephen and Rachel and says she is Mrs. Pegler. Louisa and Tom also visit. Louisa gives Stephen a small amount of money to help him on his way, while Tom lays a plot that will result in Stephen being accused of robbery.

Harthouse ingratiates himself with Louisa by revealing that he knows her brother has gambling debts. Harthouse convinces Louisa that he wishes to help Tom, but his purpose is to win over Louisa's heart for himself. Later, Tom confesses to Harthouse that he is in desperate need of money and resents his sister for not giving him more.

Bounderby reports that some money was stolen from Tom's safe at the bank. He suspects that Stephen is the culprit, since Stephen was seen lurking in the vicinity of the bank for several nights. Bounderby also suspects the mysterious old woman he has heard about. But Louisa fears that Tom might have had something to do with it.

Aided by the meddling Mrs. Sparsit, who is jealous of Louisa, Louisa and Harthouse become closer, and Louisa becomes alienated from her husband. When Bounderby is absent, Mrs. Sparsit observes Harthouse and Louisa in earnest conversation. Harthouse tells Louisa he is in love with her. Mrs. Sparsit thinks they are planning to meet in town, and she follows Louisa on the train to Coketown but then loses track of her.

Louisa confesses to her father that she hates her husband. She also confides that she may be in love with someone else, who is waiting for her to meet him. After appealing to her father for help, she faints at his feet.

Book the Third—Garnering

Louisa wakes up in her old bed at her father's house. She is comforted by her younger sister, Jane. Gradgrind is distressed about her condition and begins to doubt the wisdom of his "hard facts" philosophy.

Harthouse, who is disturbed about why Louisa has not come to meet him as planned, is confronted by Sissy at his hotel. She knows what has happened between Harthouse and Louisa, and she takes it upon herself to demand that Harthouse leave town immediately. Harthouse reluctantly complies.

In the meantime, Mrs. Sparsit has reported her suspicions to Bounderby. Summoned by Bounderby, Gradgrind refutes Mrs. Sparsit's allegations by informing him that Louisa is at his house and has no intention of acting improperly with Harthouse. Gradgrind requests that Louisa be allowed to stay a little longer at his house, but Bounderby is insulted by this suggestion. He sends Louisa's belongings along and resumes life as a bachelor.

Media Adaptations

- *Hard Times* has been recorded on audiotape by The Audio Partners. The unabridged edition (2003) is read by Martin Jarvis.

Bounderby offers a reward for the arrest of Stephen, who is then publicly denounced by Slackbridge, the union delegate. Rachel writes to Stephen, asking him to return to clear his name. She expects him within two days, but many days go by and Stephen does not appear.

Mrs. Sparsit confronts Mrs. Pegler, who turns out to be Bounderby's mother. It also transpires that Bounderby lied about his deprived childhood. He was, in fact, well provided for.

Sissy and Rachel walk in the country. By chance they find Stephen's hat, which lies near an old mine shaft. They realize that Stephen must have been walking back to Coketown when he fell down the shaft. They summon local villagers for assistance. After much preparation, two men are lowered into the shaft, and they return with Stephen, who is badly injured. He dies before he can receive proper medical attention.

Gradgrind is now sure that Tom is guilty of the robbery. Tom has disappeared, but Sissy knows he is hiding with the circus. Louisa, Sissy, and Gradgrind travel to the town where the circus is, where Tom confesses. The circus owner, Mr. Sleary, agrees to have Tom conveyed to Liverpool and then shipped to America. But Bitzer arrives and tries to take Tom back with him to Coketown. Sleary arranges to have them intercepted on the way, and so Tom escapes as planned.

Bounderby punishes Mrs. Sparsit by sending

her away to live with her relative.

Five years later, Bounderby dies of a fit in the street. Gradgrind repudiates his former philosophy and is derided by his political associates. Rachel continues to work hard and shows compassion for Stephen's wife. Lonely, Tom dies of fever on his way home to see his sister. Louisa, although she never has children of her own, is loved by Sissy's children and does her best to stimulate in others a sense of beauty and imagination.

Characters

Bitzer

Bitzer is a boy who attends Gradgrind's school and later becomes a porter at the bank. He is clearheaded and calculating, without emotion. Near the end of the novel, when Gradgrind tries to arrange for Tom's escape, Bitzer attempts to thwart their plans by taking Tom back to Coketown. He hopes to be rewarded by Bounderby, his employer, with a promotion. In this incident, Bitzer shows he has fully absorbed his education in the "hard facts" school and acts heartlessly in his own selfish interests.

Stephen Blackpool

Stephen Blackpool is a worker at the factory. He is industrious and virtuous, showing no malice to anyone despite how badly he is treated. Stephen is trapped in a bad marriage to an alcoholic wife, who makes his domestic life a nightmare. He has a loyal friend, Rachel, but they are unable to marry because Stephen cannot afford a divorce. Stephen is ostracized by the other workers at the factory because he refuses to join their union. Bounderby decides Stephen is a troublemaker and fires him. Without any means of livelihood, Stephen leaves Coketown, only to find that he has been accused of a robbery he did not commit. Returning to

Coketown to clear his name, he falls down a disused mine shaft. He dies shortly after being rescued.

Josiah Bounderby

Josiah Bounderby is one of Coketown's most important citizens. He is a rich, self-made man in his late forties, although he looks older. He is a banker, a manufacturer, and a merchant. Bounderby is an arrogant, conceited, boastful man who takes pride in endlessly repeating how he dragged himself up by his own efforts after he was abandoned by his mother as a child. He practices a kind of inverted snobbery, in which the more wretched and poor he makes his childhood out to have been, the more moral credit he can claim for himself for becoming the important, respected man he is. Bounderby has no understanding of human nature and is content to hold his bigoted opinions. He thinks all the factory workers are idlers who want a life of luxury. He badly misjudges Stephen Blackpool and has no ability to communicate with his young wife, Louisa. When she goes to stay with her father, he angrily rejects her and returns to living as a bachelor. Bounderby's ultimate humiliation comes when his mother appears and reveals in the presence of others that his claim to have been abandoned is untrue. He was in fact well provided for as a child by a loving mother.

Louisa Bounderby

Louisa Bounderby is Thomas Gradgrind's

daughter. She is an imaginative child, but she is emotionally stifled by the rigid education she receives in her father's school and household. She is strongly attached to her brother Tom. She agrees to marry Bounderby, even though she does not love him. She does this in part to please Tom, who is living at Bounderby's house and wants to see more of her. Louisa resigns herself to her fate and keeps her emotions under control. She seems to expect nothing more from life than what she receives, since her father has never allowed her to dream. Her life is disrupted when James Harthouse arouses her affections. In turmoil, she goes to stay with her father and confesses how unhappy she is. Bounderby considers that she has left him, and the marriage is in effect over, although there is no divorce. Louisa lives the rest of her life trying to encourage others to live a more balanced life than mere facts can provide.

Thomas Gradgrind

Thomas Gradgrind is a local businessman who made money in the hardware trade. He prides himself on being "eminently practical" and values only facts and figures. He raises his children according to these principles, refusing to let them indulge in "fancy." He even admonishes them when he finds them trying to peep into a circus booth. Gradgrind becomes a Member of Parliament and only begins to realize the error of his ways when he discovers how unhappy his daughter Louisa is. His misery is compounded when he learns that his son,

Tom, is a thief. Realizing that his "hard facts" philosophy is deeply flawed, he tries to amend his life, paying more attention to the virtues of faith, hope, and charity. He is then scorned by his former political associates.

Tom Gradgrind

Tom Gradgrind is Thomas Gradgrind's son and Louisa's brother. He dislikes the education he receives from his father and becomes a failure by his father's standard. Put under Bounderby's wing, he becomes a clerk at the bank, but he is lazy and also accumulates gambling debts. To escape from the debts, he steals money from the bank and tries to frame Stephen Blackpool for the crime. To escape justice, he is forced to emigrate to the United States.

James Harthouse

James Harthouse is a charming but cynical gentleman who has found no true mission in life. He has been a cavalry officer and has traveled around the world, but he always gets bored with what he is doing. He is recruited by Gradgrind for the utilitarian cause and sent to Coketown. But Harthouse only pretends to be a utilitarian and merely idles his time away. He ingratiates himself with Tom Gradgrind and tries to seduce Louisa, but when confronted by Sissy, he agrees to leave town.

Cecilia Jupe

Cecilia Jupe, known as Sissy, is a young girl whose father is a member of the circus. When her father deserts her, Gradgrind takes her into his house and allows her to attend his school. Sissy does not fare well at school because she is too much in touch with her heart and does not understand the school's emphasis on mere facts and figures. She and Louisa become friends, and when Louisa is pursued by Harthouse, Sissy confronts him and demands that he leave town.

Mr. M'Choakumchild

Mr M'Choakumchild is the teacher in Gradgrind's school. He is well trained and knowledgeable, but the narrator does not believe he is a good teacher.

Mrs. Pegler

Mrs. Pegler is Josiah Bounderby's mother. She appears mysteriously in Coketown without at first disclosing her identity. But when she meets her son, she discloses the true details of his upbringing, which he has falsified.

Rachel

Rachel is Stephen Blackpool's longtime friend. She shows great love and loyalty to him, even though she knows they will never be able to marry. She is with him when he dies.

Sissy

See Cecilia Jupe

Slackbridge

Slackbridge is the union delegate who gives a rabble-rousing speech to the factory workers. He excoriates Stephen Blackpool for not joining their union and later on is quick to condemn Stephen again when Stephen is accused of robbery.

Mr. Sleary

Mr. Sleary is the owner of the circus. He is a kindly old man who suffers from asthma and is frequently the worse for drink. His philosophy is the opposite of Gradgrind's; he believes that people cannot spend all their lives working and learning because they must also have their amusements. Near the end of the novel, he shelters Tom Gradgrind and makes arrangements for Tom to leave the country.

Mrs. Sparsit

Mrs. Sparsit is Bounderby's housekeeper. She comes from the distinguished Powler family, but a long time ago she entered a disastrous marriage and has since come down in the world. She takes a dislike to Louisa and takes great pleasure in the breakup of Louisa's marriage to Bounderby. Bounderby eventually dismisses her, and she goes to live with her irascible great aunt, Lady Scadgers.

Stephen Blackpool's Wife

Stephen Blackpool's wife is never named. She has been married to Stephen for nineteen years, but the marriage deteriorated early because of her love of drink. She remains a drunk who brings her husband nothing but misery.

Themes

Fact versus Fancy

Mr. Gradgrind's educational philosophy is based on the utilitarian idea that only facts and figures are important. This excludes all other values, especially "fancy." Everything in Gradgrind's world is based on facts, measurement, and strict order. Even his house, with its rigidly symmetrical design, reflects his principles, as do the grounds. Lawn, garden, and walkway are all "ruled straight like a botanical account-book."

Fancy, on the other hand, is embodied in the child's sense of wonder, which Gradgrind attempts to eradicate in his children. Tom and Louisa are not allowed to read poetry, learn nursery rhymes, or indulge in other childish amusements. Instead of toys, their nursery contains cabinets in which various metallurgical and mineralogical specimens are neatly arranged and labeled. Once, when Louisa began a conversation by saying, "I wonder," her father had replied, "Louisa, never wonder!" For him, all questions in life can be solved by calculation, by arithmetic. Anything that is not amenable to such analysis, that does not have a tangible reality, does not really exist.

Gradgrind's world of "hard facts" also excludes all the values of the heart. This is amusingly depicted when Louisa deliberates about how to respond to Bounderby's marriage proposal. Gradgrind invites her to consider only the facts. Regarding the thirty-year difference between her and Bounderby, Gradgrind offers some statistics. He informs her that a large proportion of marriages in England and Wales are between people of very unequal ages and that in three-quarters of these cases, the elder party is the man. Similar statistics apply, according to Gradgrind, to British possessions in India and in China. Having established these facts, Gradgrind asserts that the difference in the ages of Louisa and Bounderby virtually disappears. For Gradgrind, there is nothing else to consider. Louisa's feelings in the matter are not important.

Facts and statistics are at the heart of the curriculum in Coketown's school. This is why Sissy, who was raised in a circus family (the embodiment of fancy, according to Gradgrind), does not fare well there. The schoolmaster, the appropriately named M'Choakumchild, tries to convince her with statistics about how prosperous a town is if, out of a million inhabitants, only twenty-five starve to death in the streets each year. Sissy replies that it must be just as hard on the twenty-five, however many people there are who are not starving. Sissy always gives common sense answers that show she is in touch with the feeling level of life. She converts statistics into real people with real lives, which is not the way to flourish in Gradgrind's model school.

Topics for Further Study

- Should all students today receive an education in the arts as well as the sciences? How does cultivation of the imagination help a person succeed in life?
- How do the circus folk differ from Gradgrind and Bounderby? What are their values? Are they characters to be admired and emulated?
- Write a character sketch of Mrs. Sparsit. How does Dickens make her into a witchlike figure?
- Critics often argue that Stephen Blackpool and Rachel are not believable characters because they are too good to be true and that Bounderby is not believable because he is too bad to be true. Is there any

truth in these views? How do you react to these characters? Why do you think Dickens created them the way he did?

Gradgrind's dedication to facts does not work because it deprives people of vital aspects of their humanity. Louisa is forced to live an emotionally stifled life and finds herself trapped in a loveless marriage. Tom resents his education and says he would like to take all the facts and figures he has been taught and all the people who had taught them and blow them up with gunpowder. In Book Three, everything Gradgrind represents unravels. Louisa's marriage fails, and Tom is revealed as a thief. Such are the fruits of Gradgrind's "hard facts" approach to education.

The only person who thrives on the education he receives is Bitzer, who shows in his confrontation with Gradgrind in Book Three how well he has absorbed his lessons. When Gradgrind, trying to save Tom, asks Bitzer whether he has a heart, Bitzer replies in true Gradgrindian fashion: Since the blood cannot circulate without a heart to pump it, he certainly does have a heart. But it operates only according to the dictates of reason. Bitzer wants to take Tom back to Coketown because he expects Bounderby to reward him by promoting him at the bank. When Gradgrind tells him he has only his own interests at heart, Bitzer reminds his mentor that the whole social system is set up as a matter of self-interest. He is only repeating what he was taught. Gradgrind, to his distress, is hoisted on his own petard.

Evils of Industrialism

Dickens's critique of industrialism is apparent in his physical descriptions of Coketown and in his presentation of relations between owners and workers.

Coketown is an unnatural, blighted place, constructed according to the utilitarian philosophy that Dickens refers to as Fact. Everything in Coketown is designed to maximize industrial output. Nothing else matters. The town itself is disfigured by all the smoke that belches from the factory chimneys and which turns the red bricks of the houses black. The river has been polluted by bad-smelling dye, and the canal is black. All the houses are exactly like one another, and all the other buildings resemble one another, too. (The jail, the infirmary and the town hall all look the same.) Everything, including the people, has been reduced to drab conformity. The place runs according to clockwork; everyone's routine is the same, day after day, year after year. It is a place not fit for humans to live in. This is symbolized by the variety of crooked and stunted chimneys on the houses, which proclaim that anyone born under these roofs is likely to be stunted in some way, too.

Industrialism, with its emphasis on efficient production and nothing else, has ruined the lives of the workers in the factories, who toil long, monotonous hours, with little relief. Relations between the classes in Coketown are abysmal. The employers have a contemptuous opinion of the workers. They think the factory hands drink too much or stupefy themselves with opium. This hostile attitude is represented by Bounderby, who regards all the workers as ungrateful and restless, forever dissatisfied with their lot, even though, in his mind, they can afford to live well. Bounderby assumes the factory hands are all lazy and that anyone who complains simply wants a life of luxury, with "a coach and six, and to be fed on turtle soup and venison, with a gold spoon." He dismisses legitimate complaints as the work of external agitators.

Stephen Blackpool expresses the situation between the two groups in a nutshell when he says the bosses consider themselves "awlus right," while the workers are "awlus wrong," no matter what they say or do. Stephen regards the economic and political system in Coketown and beyond as a "muddle." He can offer no solution to the problem (and neither does Dickens), but he does tell Bounderby the approaches that will not work. It is no use the employers trying to defeat the workers by force. Nor will the economic policy of laissez faire favored by the utilitarians accomplish anything. Stephen calls this "lettin alone"; it refers to the policy of allowing market forces to dictate economic arrangements without interference by government. According to Stephen, this will only create a "black unpassable world" between the two groups. Most of all, Stephen says, it will not work to treat the workers as machines rather than as human beings with feelings and hopes. Bounderby's response to this is to fire Stephen.

Dickens, although often accused of writing a didactic work, offers no prescription for redeeming places like Coketown or changing economic systems that put men like Bounderby in charge of them. His final image is of Louisa doing what she can in her own small sphere to keep alive the hope of a balanced life, one not ruthlessly circumscribed by the worship of purely utilitarian considerations.

Style

Satire

Satire is the literary technique of exposing someone or something to ridicule. The intent is to arouse contempt or amusement in the reader. Gradgrind, M'Choakumchild, Bounderby, and Mrs. Sparsit are the principle targets of satire in *Hard Times*, as well as the powers-that-be in Coketown.

For example, in Book 1, chapter 2, the description of the rigors of M'Choakumchild's training and the long list of the subjects he has studied are not meant to impress the reader with his knowledge and wisdom. On the contrary, they are set out only to mock him, as the facetious tone suggests and as the last sentence explicitly states: "Ah, rather overdone, M'Choakumchild. If he had only learnt a little less, how infinitely better he might have taught much more!" The point is that M'Choakumchild may know a lot, but he has neither the wisdom nor the skill to know how to impart it to young minds.

Sometimes Dickens uses satiric irony, in which the satire is carried out by implying the opposite of what the surface meaning of the words states. This technique can be seen in the way Gradgrind mentally introduces himself to virtually anyone he encounters:

Thomas Gradgrind, sir. A man of realities. A man of facts and calculations. A man who proceeds upon the principle that two and two are four, and nothing over, and who is not to be talked into allowing for anything over.

The irony is that Gradgrind thinks this shows what an intelligent, "eminently practical" man he is, but of course to the reader it means the exact opposite.

Imagery

Coketown is always enveloped in clouds of smoke, which are belched out from the chimneys of houses and factories. They are described as "serpents of smoke," primarily because they trail out in a coiled shape that never uncoils. The image, which is repeated several times in the novel, suggests the ominous, life-denying quality of the industrial town, as if an evil, serpent-like spirit hovers over it. The serpent-smoke image is used in conjunction with an elephant image. The pistons of the steam engines in the factories as they move up and down are likened several times to "the head of an elephant in a state of melancholy madness," an image that gives to inanimate objects the sinister, aggressive quality of great animal power trapped in endless repetitive activity.

Symbols

Pegasus, the winged horse from Greek

mythology, is used in the novel as a symbol of fancy, as opposed to fact. The circus folk, who embody the fancy-principle, live at the Pegasus's Arms, which has a picture of Pegasus on its signboard. Inside, behind the bar, is a framed portrait of "another Pegasus," one of the circus horses, "with real gauze let in for his wings, golden stars stuck on all over him, and his ethereal harness made of red silk." The circus performers make their living by riding horses and performing feats of balance, strength, and horsemanship on them. The horses are a vital part of the entertainment that the circus offers, giving people a sense of wonder, something other than facts and figures. Horses can make the human imagination soar.

The Pegasus symbol offers a devastating comment on Gradgrind's directive to the children in class (Book 1, chapter 2), to define a horse. Bitzer offers a purely factual definition, which includes this: "Quadruped. Graminivorous. Forty teeth, namely twenty-four grinders, four eye-teeth, and twelve incisive." This definition pleases Gradgrind, but of course it excludes everything symbolized by Pegasus. The point is driven home further if the flying Pegasus is seen in light of the comment made by the government gentleman to the children in Gradgrind's class. He tells them that they would never paper a room with representations of horses because such a thing would contradict reality: "Do you ever see horses walking up and down the sides of rooms in reality—in fact?" The government gentleman cannot conceive of a horse like Pegasus, but "fancy" can.

Historical Context

Industrial Conditions

During the early nineteenth century, the use of the power loom, which had been patented in 1785, rapidly became more widespread. This had a deleterious effect on the hand loom weavers, who could not compete with the power loom and could no longer find sufficient work. By the time Dickens wrote *Hard Times*, power looms were the norm and hand weaving was almost extinct. Because of this development, weavers were gradually driven from their home-based weaving to the factories in the towns, which grew rapidly in population. The new factory workers put in ten-hour days. Conditions were often dangerous, and industrial accidents were common. This subject gave rise to a heated article written by Henry Morley and published in Dickens's own magazine, *Household Words*, in April 1854. Morley claimed that over the previous three years, there had been a hundred deaths and nearly twelve thousand accidents in factories in England. These figures were disputed by other contemporary commentators, but there is no doubt that many serious accidents did occur, often caused by unguarded machinery. In *Hard Times*, there is a reference to people being "chopped up" by machinery (Book 2, chapter 1).

Factory workers sought to protect their own

interests by joining trade unions, which were growing in power in the 1850s. But the unions often faced fierce opposition from employers. A notorious example of industrial conflict took place in Preston, a textile-manufacturing town in northwest England, not far from Dickens's fictional Coketown. In October 1853, between fifteen and sixteen thousand weavers went on strike for better pay. The mill owners responded by closing the mills. A bitter struggle ensued, in which the strikers were sustained only by contributions from union members in other manufacturing towns. Union leaders were arrested and charged with conspiracy. (This recalls Bounderby's threat in *Hard Times* to have Slackbridge and other union delegates arrested on felony charges and shipped off to penal settlements.)

Compare & Contrast

- **1850s:** The groundwork is laid for universal compulsory education. In 1858, the British government appoints a commission to inquire into the state of education. The commission recommends an increase of state grants to schools, as long as the schools pass an inspection test regarding teaching standards.

  Today: All children in Britain up to the age of sixteen must, by law, receive full-time schooling. Over 90 percent of pupils receive state-funded education; the rest choose independent schooling. National targets are set for raising literacy and numeracy standards.

- **1850s:** Workers in textile mills are so poorly paid that they are forced to send their children to work in the factories as well. Government legislation reduces working hours to ten a day; weekly work hours amount to sixty.
  Today: The British government introduces a statutory minimum wage in April 1999 to reduce exploitation of low-paid workers and to ensure greater fairness in the workplace. The maximum working week is fixed by the European Union at forty-eight hours.

- **1850s:** The laissez-faire economic philosophy advocated by the utilitarians puts faith solely in the market forces of supply and demand, believing that this will deliver the greatest benefit to the greatest number of people. Utilitarians therefore oppose government regulation of economic and industrial conditions, although this does not prevent the passing of the

Factory Acts in 1844, 1847, 1850, and 1867, regulating such things as the length of the working day.

Today: Like all modern industrial nations, Britain has long ago abandoned laissez-faire economic principles. Instead, the economy is guided by government fiscal policy, which aims to produce economic stability that cannot be produced by relying solely on market forces.

Dickens took an interest in the conflict and visited Preston to get an idea of the mood and the conditions of life there. He attended a union delegate meeting, which gave him material for the Slackbridge episodes in *Hard Times*, and in general he gained a favorable impression of the workers and their representatives, as he recorded in his article, "On Strike," which was published in *Household Words* in February, 1854. Dickens wrote in conclusion:

> [T]his strike and lock-out is a deplorable calamity. In its waste of time, in its waste of a great people's energy, in its waste of wages, in its waste of wealth that seeks to be employed, in its encroachment on the means of many thousands who are laboring from day to day… it is a great national affliction.

The Preston strikers found it increasingly difficult to survive on what they were receiving in contributions from other unions, and when the contributions began to fall off in April 1854, the strike collapsed. The strike leader was thrown into jail for debts he incurred during the strike.

Education

In 1854, there was no system of compulsory schooling in England. This was not to be established until the Elementary Education Act of 1870, the year of Dickens's death. However, there was at the time a large number of schools, differing widely in quality, methods of funding and organization, and the type of pupil who attended. The school that Gradgrind is so proud of was a non-fee-paying school for students of the lower classes, of which there were many. There was a general feeling among the educated classes that universal literacy should be achieved and that the poor should be better educated. Recognizing that teachers were often incompetent and untrained, the government had set out in the 1840s to improve teaching standards. Teacher training colleges were set up, and the first graduates emerged in 1853. In *Hard Times*, M'Choakumchild is one such newly trained teacher, although from Dickens's satirical treatment of him it is apparent that Dickens was not impressed with the results of the training program.

A review of *Hard Times*, published in the *Westminster Review* in 1854, questioned whether any school like Mr. Gradgrind's actually existed anywhere in England. The reviewer claimed that the

English educational system gave as free a rein to the imagination and the study of the arts as any in the world. Dickens, as might be expected, claimed otherwise. In a speech given in 1857, he claimed to have seen too many schools in which the imagination of the children was discouraged and the pupils trained as "little parrots and small calculating machines" ("Schools I Do Not Like"). In *Dickens and Education*, Philip Collins shows that many educators at the time expressed views similar to those of Dickens. They believed there was too much emphasis on cramming the children full of names, dates, and facts but not allowing enough time for them to digest the information. There was also plenty of complaint that the schools were failing to develop the whole child and that the teacher-training curriculum was too mechanical and tried to achieve too much in too short a period of time.

Critical Overview

When first published in 1854, *Hard Times* did not receive the same praise that was customary for Dickens's other novels. Reviewers, with a few exceptions, were reluctant to hail it as an example of his best work. Some reviewers thought the book too didactic, too intent on conveying the evils of industrialism, and lacking Dickens's customary humor. Richard Simpson, in the *Rambler*, described it as a "mere dull melodrama, in which character is caricature, sentiment tinsel, and moral (if any) unsound." On the other hand, the novel did have its defenders. Well-known social critic John Ruskin called it "in several respects the greatest [Dickens] has written," although he faulted it for exaggerating the characters of Bounderby and Stephen Blackpool, making the former into a monster and the latter too perfect. But Edwin P. Whipple, in the *Atlantic Monthly*, took issue with Ruskin's positive assessment and accused Dickens of exaggerating the evils he opposed. According to Whipple, Dickens made "rash and hasty judgments on the whole government of Great Britain.... Heoverlooked uses, in order to fasten on abuses."

The status of *Hard Times* in the canon of Dickens's work has been problematic ever since. For nearly a century, it was in general regarded as one of Dickens's minor and less successful novels (although it was championed by no less a critic than Bernard Shaw). In the mid-twentieth century, however, the novel underwent a reevaluation. This was stimulated by one of the century's most influential critics, F. R. Leavis, who claimed in 1948 that *Hard Times* was a "masterpiece" and Dickens's finest novel. According to Leavis, *Hard Times* was different from other Dickens novels in the sense that Dickens's social criticisms are casual and incidental. But in *Hard Times*, "he is for once possessed by a comprehensive vision, one in which the inhumanities of Victorian civilization are seen as fostered and sanctioned by a hard philosophy, the aggressive formulation of an inhumane spirit."

This reassessment generated some controversy, and a number of critics attempted to refute Leavis's claims. Since then, *Hard Times* has had its share of detractors and defenders. It is fair to state that the novel will probably never be most readers' favorite work by Dickens. However, it seems unlikely also that the novel will fall into the neglect it had suffered before Leavis. As Paul Edward Gray states in his "Introduction" to *Twentieth Century Interpretations of "Hard Times": A Collection of Critical Essays*, "If... *Hard Times* is a limited success, it is also an endlessly fascinating work, fascinating both despite and because of Dickens's ambivalence toward the demands of art and argument."

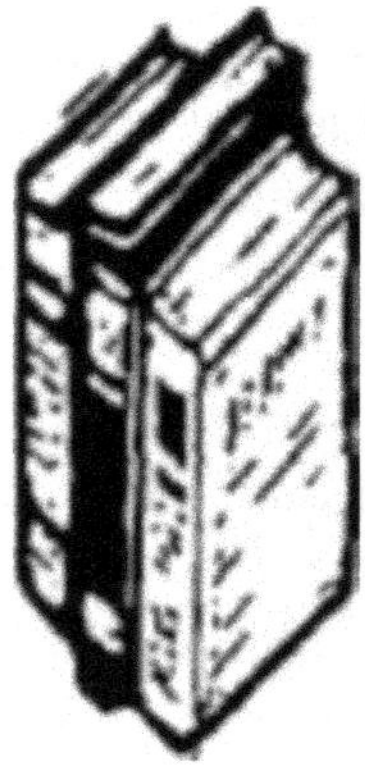

What Do I Read Next?

- Dickens's *Great Expectations* (first published in serial form in 1860–1861) tells the story of young Pip and his mysterious benefactor. It has always been one of Dickens's most popular and critically acclaimed novels.
- *What Jane Austen Ate and Charles Dickens Knew: From Fox Hunting to Whist, The Facts of Daily Life in Nineteenth-Century England* (1994), by Daniel Pool, is a guide to Victorian life. The first part covers topics such as marriage, law, class, and Parliament; the second part is a dictionary of terms that commonly occur in Victorian novels and need to be explained to the modern

reader.

- *Mary Barton: A Tale of Manchester Life*, the first novel by Elizabeth Gaskell, is based on a real event, the murder in 1831 of a progressive mill owner in Manchester, England. The story follows the life of Mary Barton through adolescence, love, and marriage. Set in Manchester (which was Dickens's model for Coketown) from 1837 to 1842, it presents a sympathetic portrait of working-class people as they struggle through the period known as the "hungry forties."
- *The World of Charles Dickens* (1970), by Angus Wilson, is regarded by many as the finest one-volume study of Dickens's life and work. Wilson is a novelist, and he writes with vigor, penetration, and astute judgment. The book is illustrated with a large number of engravings and color reproductions.

Sources

Collins, Philip, *Charles Dickens: The Critical Heritage*, Routledge and Kegan Paul, 1971, pp. 300–21.

——, *Dickens and Education*, Macmillan, 1963, pp. 144–59.

Dickens, Charles, *Hard Times*, Norton Critical Edition, edited by George Ford and Sylvàre Monod, W. W. Norton, 1966.

——, "The Murdered Person," in *"Gone Astray" and Other Papers from "Household Words," 1851–59*, The Dent Uniform Edition of Dickens's Journalism, edited by Michael Slater, Vol. 3, Ohio State University Press, 1999, pp. 396–402.

——, "On Strike," in *Hard Times*, Norton Critical Edition, edited by George Ford and Sylvàre Monod, W. W. Norton, 1966, pp. 286–99, originally published in *Household Words*, February 11, 1854.

——, "Schools I Do Not Like," in *Hard Times*, Norton Critical Edition, edited by George Ford and Sylvàre Monod, W. W. Norton, 1966, pp. 310–11, originally given as a speech, November 5, 1857.

Gray, Paul Edward, ed., *Twentieth Century Interpretations of "Hard Times": A Collection of Critical Essays*, Prentice-Hall, 1969.

House, Humphry, and John House, *Dickens World*, 2d ed., Oxford University Press, 1965, pp. 203–11.

Leavis, F. R., "*Hard Times*—An Analytic Note," in *Hard Times*, Norton Critical Edition, edited by George Ford and Sylvàre Monod, W. W. Norton, 1966, pp. 339–59, originally published in *The Great Tradition*, 1948, pp. 227–48.

Morley, Henry, "Ground in the Mill," in *Hard Times*, Norton Critical Edition, edited by George Ford and Sylvàre Monod, W. W. Norton, 1966, pp. 299–301, originally published in *Household Words*, April 22, 1854.

Review of *Hard Times*, in *Hard Times*, Norton Critical Edition, edited by George Ford and Sylvàre Monod, W. W. Norton, 1966, pp. 286–99, originally published in *Westminster Review*, 1854.

Ruskin, John, Review of *Hard Times*, in *Charles Dickens: The Critical Heritage*, edited by Philip Collins, Routledge and Kegan Paul, 1971, pp. 303–04, originally published in *Cornhill Magazine*, August 1860.

Shanley, Mary Lyndon, *Feminism, Marriage, and the Law in Victorian England, 1850–1895*, Princeton University Press, 1989, pp. 22–48.

Simpson, Richard, Review of *Hard Times*, in *Charles Dickens: The Critical Heritage*, edited by Philip Collins, Routledge and Kegan Paul, 1971, pp. 303–04, originally published in *Rambler*, October 1854.

Whipple, Edwin P., Review of *Hard Times*, in *Charles Dickens: The Critical Heritage*, edited by Philip Collins, Routledge and Kegan Paul, 1971, pp.

351–21, originally published in *Atlantic Monthly*, March 1877.

Further Reading

Dyson, A. E., *The Inimitable Dickens: A Reading of the Novels*, Macmillan, 1970, pp. 183–202.

> Dyson argues that *Hard Times*, Dickens's "angriest" novel, differs from his other novels because it is devoid of hope. There is no happy ending for any of the characters.

Monod, Sylvàre, *Dickens the Novelist*, University of Oklahoma Press, 1968, pp. 440–52, 456–65.

> Monod discusses *Hard Times* and *A Tale of Two Cities* as examples of the least Dickensian of Dickens's novels. Monod faults Dickens for not providing a positive element in his social criticism and for the inconsistency in his thinking.

Nelson, Harland S., *Charles Dickens*, Twayne's English Authors Series, No. 314 Twayne, 1981, pp. 197–201.

> Nelson discusses *Hard Times* in the context of the limitations of reason and intellect, namely that reason excludes love, which is needed for any solution to the world's problems.

Spector, Stephen J., "Monsters of Metonymy: *Hard Times* and Knowing the Working Class," in *Charles Dickens*, edited and with an introduction by Harold

Bloom, Modern Critical Views series, Chelsea House, 1987, pp. 229–44.

Spector examines what he calls Dickens's failure to create a convincing portrayal of industrial workers, which he attributes to Dickens's faith in the power of language. While analyzing the novel's failings, Spector also praises its moral and intellectual honesty.

Lightning Source UK Ltd.
Milton Keynes UK
UKHW020642280223
417789UK00016B/515